The Rule-Breaking Letterer's Workbook

Prompts & Inspiration for Embracing Imperfection

HUYEN DINH

CHRONICLE BOOKS
SAN FRANCISCO

ISBN 978-1-7972-1554-9

Manufactured in China.

Design by Kayla Ferriera.
Typeset in Circular Pro, Wildside, Lava Lamp,
and Palmer Lake Print.

10 9 8 7 6 5 4 3 2 1

Chronicle books and gifts are available at
special quantity discounts to corporations,
professional associations, literacy programs,
and other organizations. For details and
discount information, please contact our
premiums department at corporatesales@
chroniclebooks.com or at 1-800-759-0190.

Chronicle Books LLC
680 Second Street
San Francisco, California 94107
www.chroniclebooks.com

Hi there!

Dear Artists (especially the anxious ones),

Before you get freaked out seeing all these blank pages, keep reading. It will get better.

This is not just a sketchbook but a safe place for you to create whatever you want.

Do you have sketchbook anxiety? Remember that excitement when you bought a new sketchbook? But then you got home, opened it, stared at the blank page, and felt paralyzed. You felt like the page was mocking you, saying, "Why should you bother to draw in here? It won't be that great anyway."

"Wait, maybe it's right," you told yourself and closed your sketchbook. It rested in peace on the shelf for the next few years.

The good news is that this doesn't only happen to you. Other creatives face blank-page anxiety, too (*yes*, the struggle is real). Even I, when writing this for you, took some time to get past the first page. No worries, there is a cure for this.

The root of the problem is that you think your drawing is not good enough, and you compare yourself to other artists who have beautiful sketches (that look like your finals). Ouch! The truth hurts.

What if we learned to embrace our pretty "ugly" sketches? They have their charm, too, ya know.

This sketchbook is made *for you*. You don't have to show it to anyone, except maybe your furry friends, your plants, or your imaginary friend. Even if you want to keep it to yourself, that's totally fine, too.

I got tons of pages for you: blanks, easy-to-follow prompts, and "Do the damn thing" kinds of quotes to keep you company, to encourage you to laugh off your fear of blank-page anxiety, to help you grow into loving your ugly sketches, and to inspire you to create more.

Sketchbooks are not meant to be perfect. They are places for you to explore ideas freely. They help document your progress and bring good memories when you look back at them. Like that scribbled sketch you drew when you woke up in the middle of the night and thought of an awesome idea that totally makes no sense to anyone but you. Think of this as a journal for your artistic journey.

And remember, no judgments here. You're in a safe place. Now go (to the next page, not like abandoning the sketch-book) and let your creativity run wild.

AFFIRMATIONS FOR A POSITIVE MINDSET

Before you start your creative journey, let's strengthen your mindset. We all struggle with impostor syndrome and that's totally normal. There might not be a way to get rid of it completely, but we can learn how to rewire our brains. Every time you need a reminder, this note will be here for you:

Dear Artists,

Your art may not change the world.
But it simply does matter,
Because if you can change one person's day,
That person can change another person's day.
And just like that,
The world can be a better place
Because of you.

Everything is connected.
You might not see a direct impact,
But indirectly, you make a difference.
Even if it's a tiny difference,
It still counts.

We need your creations in this world.
Your creative journey is just beginning.

Keep creating, my friends!

YOU ARE WHAT YOU THINK

HOW TO USE THIS BOOK:

There is no rule for using this book. This workbook will be the place to embrace your ugly sketches and to store your feelings. It will also be your cheerleader, encouraging you to create more.

Draw, write, scribble on any page you like.

Most importantly, *draw whatever you want*! (Your creation is safe with me.)

A BREAKUP LETTER TO PERFECTION

One of the biggest things that hold people back from creating is thinking, "My art is not perfect." So let's break up with Perfection!

Dear Perfection,

I remember the first time I met you. You were stunning and flawless. At first, our relationship felt like it was the most perfect thing that had ever happened to me, but lately, everything has felt wrong.

Keeping up with all your expectations makes me feel exhausted. My quirkiness, my differences, my so-called flaws have to stay hidden so I can look good with you, Perfection. I have been trying to be someone I'm not. I'm afraid to make mistakes when I'm around you and feel like I'm walking on eggshells. I'm desperate for your validation all the time.

I cannot spend a day without you. But this attachment to you is driving me crazy.

It sounds cliché that it's not you, it's me, but it's true. I've come to the realization that I deserve to be loved the way I am, not the way I'm supposed to be.

That's why it pains me to say goodbye, but it is better this way. I wish you all the best.

Your imperfect ex,

[Your name]

ARE YOU AFRAID THAT WHAT YOU CREATE IS NOT GOOD ENOUGH?

No worries, we all have to start somewhere. Let me show you my first lettering sketch (from April 2014).

OK, OK, I know what you're thinking. It might not look impressive to you, but I was really proud of myself for making my first lettering piece ever.

Fast forward to now: I'm here writing a book and a workbook to encourage you to draw. It all starts with practice. If I'm brave enough to print and show my first sketch to millions of people, you can do it, too. I lifted the weight for ya and filled this first page. Now it's your turn to do it. I will be here cheering you on throughout.

Here is the secret of how to start creating NOW, when you don't know where to start:

GOT A PENCIL?
YOU'RE READY NOW.

Before impostor syndrome comes to visit, write down the first thing that comes to your mind right now (even if it's silly). Now letter it. This exercise will help you with the creative flow.

TIP

Don't overthink this.

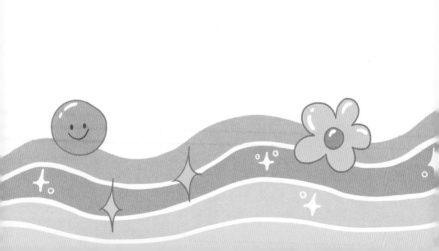

WHERE DO YOU WANT TO GO FOR A VACAY?

Letter the place where you want to be right now.

MY TURN

MY HOME COUNTRY IS VIETNAM, AND I WOULD WANT TO BE THERE FOR A VACAY ANYTIME.

TIP

It can be a country, a city, or even home. Once you pick a place, draw icons related to that place around your lettering.

SLOW DOWN
(LIFE IS NOT A RACE)

LETTER WHO YOU ARE.

Before you can fight your self-doubt, it's important to know who you are as a person as well as an artist. Create the lettering piece about YOU; think of it as your short Wikipedia entry.

TIPS

If you don't know where to start, ask yourself these questions:

What do you enjoy creating?

What are three strengths that you have? (You can be silly here. For example, I'm good at makeup and lettering, so lettering is like a type makeover for me.)

MY TURN

Huyền Đinh IS A VIETNAMESE MILLENNIAL Letterer who gives TYPE MAKEOVERS BY BLENDING Colorful PALETTES WITH SARCASM

YOUR TURN

HELLO

HOW MANY WAYS CAN YOU DRAW ONE WORD OR LETTER?

Pick one word or even one letter to draw as many variations of as you can. This exercise will help you push the limit, and you may be surprised by how far you can go.

MY TURN

I PICKED THE PHRASE "GOOD VIBES."

YOUR TURN

TIPS

I know it will get hard once you get to the fifth version but keep pushing; you can do it. It's like when you are at the last rep of working out: You feel like your body is giving up, but if you can strengthen your mind, you can finish those sets.

If you have my book, *How to Be a Rule-Breaking Letterer*, refer back to chapters 2 and 6 for tips on how to push the styles.

CREATE YOUR OWN JUICE.

If you could drink a magical juice every day
to help you create, what would it be?

MY TURN

I NEED THIS "BE U"
JUICE EVERY DAY TO
BE MORE CONFIDENT.

TIP

Think outside the box, beyond
orange or grape juice. Maybe
it can be confidence juice; take
no BS juice; I'm awesome juice.
Packaging types can be a can,
a cup, a carton, etc.

YOUR TURN

OVERCOME THE LIMITING BELIEFS THAT HOLD YOU BACK FROM CREATING.

Rewrite your limiting beliefs as positive affirmations.

MY TURN

LIMITING BELIEF: NO ONE IS GOING TO BUY MY BOOK.

REWRITE: I WROTE THIS BOOK BECAUSE I WANT TO HELP ARTISTS OVERCOME THEIR STRUGGLES. I HAVE A LOYAL AUDIENCE, AND EVEN MY PUBLISHER BELIEVES IN ME ENOUGH TO SIGN WITH ME. TOGETHER WE CAN MAKE SURE THIS BOOK GOES TO PEOPLE WHO NEED IT.

LIMITING BELIEF: NO ONE IS GOING TO LIKE MY ART.

REWRITE: CREATING ART MAKES ME HAPPY AND IF SOMEONE DOESN'T LIKE IT, IT'S OK. WHOEVER FEELS RESONANCE WILL APPRECIATE IT.

TIP

Limiting beliefs are thoughts that prevent us from being our best selves. To tackle your limiting beliefs, you first need to identify them. Then recognize that they're just beliefs. After that, you have the power to change them.

YOUR TURN

STAY IN SHAPE!

Pick a short quote and fit the lettering into a shape.
(Check pages 138–139 in my book, How to Be a
Rule-Breaking Letterer, *for more instruction.)*

MY TURN

YOU CAN'T PLEASE EVERYONE YOU'RE NOT SRIRACHA

—@MISSHUYENDINH

TIPS

Food is always a fun theme to do. Choose a simple shape with a lot of room to fit your lettering: ice cream, donut, juice bottle, coffee cup. Avoid complicated and pointy shapes like snowflakes; it might be hard to fit your lettering inside them.

YOUR TURN

YOU'RE

AMAZING

LET'S DO SOME PUNNY LETTERING.

Who doesn't love a good pun? Show off your humor by lettering your favorite food pun. You can combine illustrations and lettering for this piece.

TIPS

Some ideas for you to get started with:

Soup-er hero

You're the coolest (with ice cream illustration)

It's Fry-day!

Donut worry, be happy.

MY TURN

HOW ARE YOU FEELING TODAY?

Fill in the blank:

I'M FEELING

TODAY

Now letter the word you wrote to describe your feelings.

LETTER ALL THE FEELS.

Embrace your feelings. Let them all out.

IT'S OK TO FEEL
SAD · CONFUSED · SCARED · RIGHT NOW
DON'T feel GUILTY ABOUT your FEELINGS
it's OK TO not be PRODUCTIVE
TAKE A BREAK
IT WILL GET BETTER

TIPS

Emotions are complex and maybe you're feeling all sorts of feelings right now beyond one word. Write down all your emotions. Now letter those feelings in a creative way to let them out.

YOUR TURN

WHAT IS YOUR MOTTO IN LIFE?

Letter words you want to live by.

MY TURN

SINCE MENTAL HEALTH IS MY PRIORITY, I CAME UP WITH THIS MOTTO: "WORK LESS, REST OFTEN."

TIPS

You can choose an inspirational quote, or you can totally make one up as well.

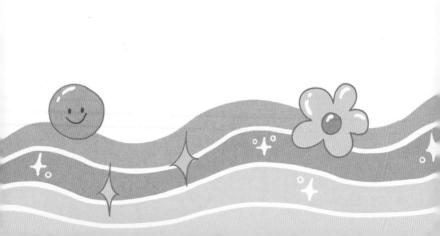

HOLIDAYS PUN

It's always fun to put a twist on traditional holiday sayings.
Pick a popular quote and swap one word out to make it yours.

TIPS

Stick with one holiday first. Write down a list of quotes related to it. Try to see which word you can make a pun on. For example:

"Ho Ho Ho" can become "Ho Ho Home for the Holidays" (since we stayed home during the COVID-19 pandemic).

"Merry Christmas" can become "Merry Stress-mas" (a lot of people get stressed out during the holiday).

YOUR TURN

START YOUR "IDEAS BANK."

Are you struggling with "What should I letter?" Maybe you can start an "Ideas Bank" to save up all your ideas here (even the silly ones). Then, once you're rich with ideas, you won't run short. Write your idea on each coin.

TIPS

If you can't think of anything, it's OK. Just come back here when you have an inside joke with a friend or come across a favorite quote in a show or podcast, and deposit it in your bank.

FEELING UNINSPIRED? IT'S OK, CLOSE THIS NOTEBOOK AND
GO HAVE SOME FUN. I WILL BE HERE WHEN YOU GET BACK.

CREATE A BEAUTY PRODUCT.

Imagine creating your own beauty product to make you feel better. What would you make? Letter and illustrate your go-to product that would enhance your day.

MY TURN

CC (CREATIVE CONFIDENCE) CREAM IS AN IMPOSTOR SYNDROME—FREE MAKEUP WITH FULL COVERAGE FOR A CONFIDENT FINISH. SUITABLE FOR ALL SKIN TYPES. APPLY AS OFTEN AS NEEDED.

CC
CREAM

CREATIVE CONFIDENCE CREAM

ALL SKIN TYPES

FULL COVERAGE

CONCEAL IMPOSTER SYNDROME

* APPLY AS MANY LAYERS AS NEEDED

WHAT BRINGS YOU JOY?

Letter and illustrate what makes your day better.

TIP

Happiness is all around you, even in the simple things in life. Write down the list of things that bring you joy: making coffee, enjoying the sun, or even smelling fresh laundry. Then pick one from the list to letter.

WHY SO SERIOUS?

Letter a funny quote that makes you giggle. Come back to this page when you have a bad day.

MY TURN

DON'T Half-Ass ANYTHING use Your Full ASS

TIP

Your quote can be from your favorite comedy show or inside jokes with your friends.

YOUR TURN

BE NICE TO YOURSELF.

Oops, I did it again! I was mean to myself.
If you have been hard on yourself, it's time to
say something nice to yourself. Letter what
you want to say on the mirror.

TIP

Here are some nice things
to say to yourself:

✦ I'm awesome.

✦ I'm strong.

✦ I'm unique.

✦ I'm brave.

✦ I'm grateful.

✦ I'm enough.

THE WAY YOU SPEAK TO YOURSELF MATTERS

AND THE AWARD GOES TO . . .

Draw an award for yourself. This will help you
know what your special strengths are. For example,
I can sleep through my ten alarms every morning.
It's a special talent.

YOUR TURN

TIPS

There are different types of awards: trophies, medals, ribbons, and more. Here are some ideas for you:

✦ Best Napper

✦ The World's Best Overthinker

✦ Queen of Sensitive Souls

✦ #1 Noodle Doodler

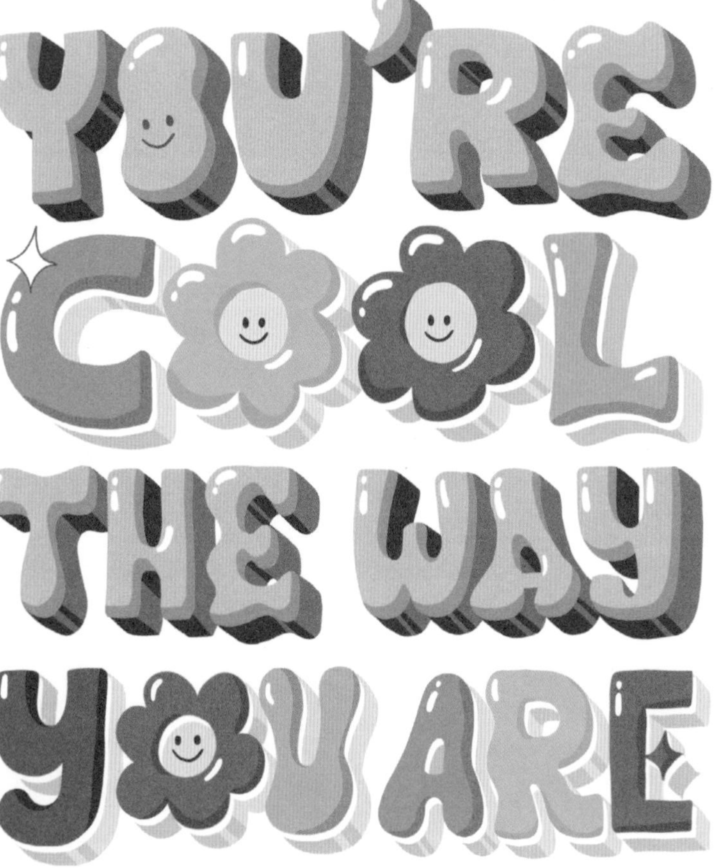
YOU'RE COOL THE WAY YOU ARE

CELEBRATE YOUR WINS
(EVEN THE TEENY-TINY ONES).

Good job on giving yourself a big award in the last
assignment but don't forget about your small wins. Fill
them in these star bursts. A small win can be as simple
as having the courage to show your work to your
friends when you usually hide it away.

SET YOUR FEEL-GOOD REMINDER.

In this hustling time, we often forget to take breaks. By resting, we can recharge, which is the most productive thing to do. So fill in this blank reminder with a message to help you relax and create better.

Reminder

♥   OK

WHAT'S ON YOUR SELF-CARE CHECKLIST?

To create better, you need to take care of yourself first, physically and mentally. Fill in the rest of this list and check in as needed.

SELF-CARE CHECKLIST

☐

☐

☐

☐

☐

☐

☐

☐

☐

☐

☐

Give yourself some peace of mind by being present—letter in the blank.

BE PROUD OF YOUR ROOTS.

What is your heritage? Fill in the blank "_____ & Proud" and letter that phrase.

MY TURN

WHEN I FIRST CAME TO THE UNITED STATES, I USED TO BE ASHAMED OF BEING ASIAN BECAUSE IT MADE ME FEEL TOO DIFFERENT FROM THE REST OF THE CROWD. NO MATTER HOW I TRIED TO AMERICANIZE, I COULD NEVER BE AN AMERICAN. THEN I REALIZED THAT I DIDN'T NEED TO FIT IN AND I SHOULD EMBRACE WHO I AM. HI, I'M A VIET GIRL AND I'M PROUD OF IT. WHERE ARE YOU FROM?

YASSS!

WHAT WOULD BE ON YOUR SHELF-LOVE?

Letter the book titles you want on your shelf to show yourself some love.

SHELF-LOVE

NOTE TO SELF.

In case you need a pick-me-up message, letter a positive note for yourself here.

~~~~~~~~~

TIPS

For example:

✦ Remember to breathe.

✦ Your feelings are valid.

✦ You don't need anyone's approval.

✦ You're not behind.

NOTE TO SELF

CREATE YOUR OWN FUTURE.

You have the power to write your own narrative. On this crystal ball, letter what your ideal future would look like in five years.

PERMISSION SLIP.

Do you feel guilty when you do things to take care of yourself? Let go of the guilt and make your own slip.

MY TURN

PERMISSION SLIP

I, _____ , GIVE YOU, _____ ,
OFFICIAL PERMISSION TO:

- ☐ Get out and have some fun
- ☐ Say "NO" sometimes
- ☐ Unplug & unwind
- ☐ Schedule a little "me time"
- ☐ Cozy up with a good book
- ☐ Sleep in a bit
- ☐ Call me for anything
- ☐
- ☐

DATE: _____   SIGNATURE: _____

EMBRACE IMPERFECTION.

What is the one quirky trait that you always try to change because it is considered imperfect by others? Embrace it by lettering it out loud. Fill that trait in this blank name tag.

MY TURN

OVERTHINKING CAN BE A NEGATIVE TRAIT IN OTHER PEOPLE'S VIEWS. HOWEVER, I REALIZE THAT NO MATTER HOW HARD I TRY, I CANNOT CHANGE WHO I AM. SO WHY NOT EMBRACE IT? THAT'S WHY I CREATED THIS DESIGN.

HELLO I'M A *Professional* OVERTHINKER

YOUR TURN

HELLO I'M A

CREATE YOUR OWN CLOSED SIGN.

What do you need a break from? Letter your sign below.

MY TURN

I TRY TO TAKE A SCREEN BREAK WEEKLY TO TAKE CARE OF MY MENTAL HEALTH, SO I CREATED THIS SIGN.

YOUR TURN

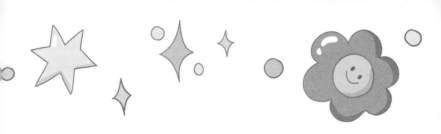

MY TURN

Mom
YOU WERE
Right
(ABOUT EVERYTHING)

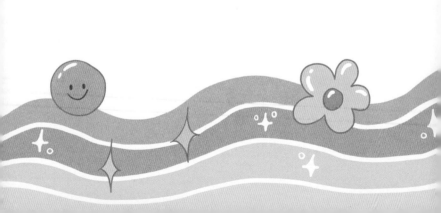

PICK A MEME AND LETTER.

Everyone loves memes; they're so relatable and funny.
So why not make one into a lettering piece?

MY TURN

*THIS ONE NEVER GETS OLD
IF YOU'RE A MILLENNIAL.*

YOUR TURN

LET IT GO.

You have to leave behind what's holding you back in order to move forward.

So write down a list below and letter what you want to leave behind in this emotional baggage.

BEING U IS YOUR SUPERPOWER

YAAAY, YOU MADE IT
TO THE LAST PAGE.

THIS IS ONLY THE BEGINNING
OF YOUR ARTISTIC JOURNEY.

DON'T STOP HERE.

YASS
inspire
Hii
LOVE
SLAY
FELT CUTE
MOOD
CREATE
LOVE
DREAM
GOOD VIBES
Hii